Conter

Birthday girl *John Escott*	2
Painting faces *Theresa Heine*	8
David's party *May Smith*	10
Seven *Traditional*	21
Calling names *Irene Rawnsley*	22
No problem at all *Frances Usher*	24

Birthday girl

Carly liked to tell people about her birthday.

"It's my birthday on Friday," she said.

"Is it?" said Mr Ditano. He put some bananas in his shop window and smiled.

"It's my birthday on Friday," said Carly.

"That's exciting," said Mrs Hill, in the cake shop.

"It's my birthday on Friday," said Carly.

"How exciting," said Mr James. He looked up at the sky. "But I have to go and fly my aeroplane now."

"It's my birthday on Friday," said Carly.

"Birthdays are exciting," said Tom MacDonald. He was painting the fence by the park.

3

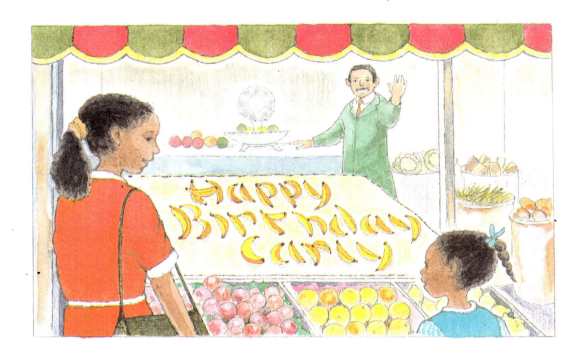

When Friday came, there was no birthday message from Mr Ditano, or Mrs Hill, or Mr James, or Tom MacDonald.

"Did they forget?" she said to Mum.

But Carly got a surprise when they went past Mr Ditano's shop.

"Oh, look!" she said. "He didn't forget!"

There was a message in the window.

It said **Happy Birthday, Carly** – in bananas!

There was another surprise at Mrs Hill's cake shop.

"Look at that cake in the window!" laughed Carly. "It says **Happy Birthday, Carly** on it!"

"I know," said Mum. She smiled. "It's for your birthday tea."

Carly got her next surprise when she saw the fence by the park. Tom was painting **Happy Birthday, Carly**.

He waved.

"Have a good birthday!" he called to Carly.

But the BIG surprise came when Carly got to school. She and the children looked up and saw Mr James's little aeroplane – and a message in the sky! **Happy Birthday, Carly**, it said.

"Now all the people in the town know it's my birthday!" laughed Carly.

Painting faces

Funny faces,

Fat and thin,

Have you put the eyebrows in?

Noses pointed, lips are blue,

This one looks a bit like you.

Theresa Heine

David's party

David was playing in the garden and Dad was trying to cut the grass. Then he called David.

"David, will you go and telephone Mr Small and ask him if I can borrow his garden shears, please?" said Dad.

"All right," said David, and off he went into the house.

"Now, who did Dad want me to telephone?" he thought. "Oh yes. It was Mr Tall." So he telephoned Mr Tall and asked him if Dad could borrow his garden chairs.

"Why does your Dad want to borrow my garden chairs?" asked Mr Tall.

"I don't know," said David. "Perhaps we're going to have a party."

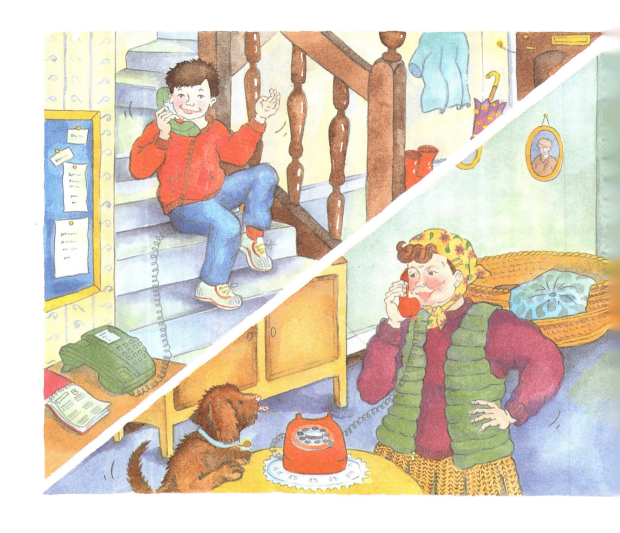

"All right," said Mr Tall. "I'll bring the chairs round, but go and telephone Mrs Green and ask her if you can borrow her table."

So David went to look for the telephone number.

"Now, who did Mr Tall want me to telephone?" he thought. "Oh yes. It was Mrs Brown." So he telephoned Mrs Brown and asked her if Dad could borrow her stable.

"Why does your Dad want to borrow my stable?" asked Mrs Brown.

"I don't know," said David. "We're having a party. Perhaps our garden is too small for a party."

"All right," said Mrs Brown. "I'll get the stable ready, but go and telephone Mr James and ask him for some big table cloths."

So David went to look for the telephone number.

"Now, who did Mrs Brown want me to telephone?" he thought. "Oh yes. It was Mr Jones." So he telephoned Mr Jones and asked him if Dad could borrow some big plates and mops.

"Why does your Dad want to borrow some big plates and mops?" asked Mr Jones.

"I don't know," said David. "We're going to have a party in Mrs Brown's stable. Perhaps the plates are to put food on and the mops are to mop the stable."

"All right," said Mr Jones. "I'll bring them round, but go and telephone Mr Baker and ask him to bring some bin bags."

"All right," said David, and he went to look for the telephone number.

"Now, who did Mr Jones want me to telephone?" he thought. "Oh yes. It was the baker." So he telephoned the baker and asked him to bring some big buns.

"We're going to have a party in Mrs Brown's stable and Mr Jones is going to bring some mops and plates," he said. "Perhaps the buns are to go on the plates."

"All right," said the baker. "I'll bring the buns round. Now go and get ready for the party."

So David went to get ready.

When he came down, Dad was waiting for him.

"What have you been doing, David?" he asked.

"Mr Tall has brought me some chairs. Mrs Brown has telephoned to say that her stable is ready. Mr Jones has brought some mops and plates and the baker has brought lots of buns! All I wanted to do was cut my grass!"

So David told Dad all about his telephone calls.

"Oh dear," said Dad. "I wanted to borrow some shears, not some chairs. What are we going to do with all these things?"

"I know," said David. "Let's have a party after all!"

Seven

One for sorrow

Two for joy

Three for a girl

Four for a boy

Five for silver

Six for gold

Seven for a secret

Never told!

Traditional

Calling names

I call my brother

Waggle Ears, Banana Boots

and Nobble Nose.

He calls me Mop Head,

Turnip Top,

Potato Pie and Twinkle Toes.

I call him Weed,

he calls me Wimp

then Mum comes in the door.

She calls us Double Trouble,

then we're both

good friends once more.

Irene Rawnsley

No problem at all

Adam had a bad habit. It was a big problem. He liked to call people names.

"Hello, Pigtails," he would say to Lucy. "All right, are you, Pigtails?"

"That boy Adam and his names," said Lucy. "He annoys me."

"Me too," said Billy. "He calls me Silly Billy."

"He calls me Rabbit," said Ranjit.

Elly Jenkins said, "He calls me Jelly Enkins. Adam is a pain. He always says silly things. We must try to stop him."

They all sat down on the grass.

"How can we stop him?" asked Ranjit.

"Let's tell the teacher," said Lucy.

"No need for that," said Elly Jenkins.

"Let's call Adam names," said Billy. "Very silly names. See how he likes it."

Adam came running by.

"Rabbit, Rabbit," he laughed. "Silly Billy and Rabbit."

"Let's hit him," said Ranjit.

"No," said Elly Jenkins. "That would be as bad as he is. Let's try to think of something clever. We must stop him."

They thought and thought. Adam came running by again.

"Jelly Enkins, Jelly Enkins," he called. "What are you all doing? Can I sit with you all, Jelly Enkins?"

Then he went red and ran away. He wanted to be friends but he didn't know how.

At last Elly Jenkins said, "I know what we can do."

Every play-time after that, the children sat by the fence and talked. Sometimes they laughed. Adam didn't know what to think. When they talked, what was it about?

"What's going on, Pigtails?" he asked Lucy one day. "Is it something exciting?" Lucy did not answer. She just smiled.

"Tell me, Silly Billy," said Adam. "Go on."

"No, Adam," said Billy.

"You'll tell me, Rabbit," said Adam.

"I won't," said Ranjit. "Not if you always call us silly names. It annoys us and we don't like it. Do we?" he asked the others.

"No," said Lucy.

"No," said Billy.

"No," said Elly Jenkins. "We don't have silly names in our club."

"Club?" Adam asked. "What club?"

"Our new club," said Elly Jenkins. "You would not want to be in it, Adam." She sat down.

"I can be in it if I like," said Adam. "Why not?"

"You like silly names," said Lucy. "We have club names, good names. You would not like it."

"I would," said Adam. He sat down next to Elly. "I would like that. I could be in your club and meet you by the fence every play-time."

Elly Jenkins looked round at the others.

"Shall we tell him our club names?" she asked.

"Well ..." said Lucy.

"Well ..." said Billy.

"Well ..." said Ranjit.

"If I remember not to call you names again," said Adam, "will you tell me?"

"All right," said Lucy. "If you are sure you won't forget, we'll tell you. Mine is Lion. Because I'm brave."

"Mine is Fox," said Billy. "Quick, clever. Not silly."

"Mine is Horse," said Ranjit. "Always running. Never tired."

"And what is your club name, Elly Jenkins?" asked Adam.

"Mine is Tiger," she said.

"What can my name be?" asked Adam.

"You'll think of something," said Elly Jenkins. "You are so good at names, Adam. You'll have no problem. No problem at all."